Theodore Thornton Munger

Character through inspiration and other papers

Theodore Thornton Munger

Character through inspiration and other papers

ISBN/EAN: 9783741132346

Manufactured in Europe, USA, Canada, Australia, Japa

Cover: Foto ©Andreas Hilbeck / pixelio.de

Manufactured and distributed by brebook publishing software (www.brebook.com)

Theodore Thornton Munger

Character through inspiration and other papers

CHARACTER THROUGH INSPIRATION,

And Other Papers.

By T. T. Munger, D.D.,
Minister of the United Church in New Haven, Conn., U.S.A.

> "The true calling of a Christian is not to do extraordinary things, but to do ordinary things in an extraordinary way."—St. Cyran.

LONDON: JAMES CLARKE & CO.,
13 & 14, Fleet Street. 1897.

Contents.

	PAGE
Character through Inspiration	1
Rest through Humility	24
Nearness the Secret of Power	37
How to Live in the World	54
Character as Four-Fold	73
Pity as Wisdom	97
Reigning and Serving	118

Character through Inspiration.

> The light of the body is the eye; therefore, when thine eye is single, thy whole body also is full of light.
>
> If thy whole body therefore be full of light, having no part dark, the whole shall be full of light, as when the bright shining of a candle doth give thee light.

LIGHT is the plaything of great minds. It is the one thing in nature they most love and like to use, and always in a free and glad way. It is the best illustration to be found in the natural world of what goes on in the world of the spirit; and if, as seems probable, there is some point where matter and spirit touch and pass into each other, it is in *light*. It is not matter, but is simply a form of motion or activity; nor is it spirit, but it stands at the gateway through which matter and spirit pass and repass.

The reason why great minds so use it is that it is the chief medium for supplying their minds with its food. Light tells them all they know. Hence all their speech of it is gladsome and grateful; they linger on it and recur to it, and never tire of it. This note of gladness can be heard in our Lord's use of it. He speaks of it with exultation. We see and feel the morning when He names it. And here, even, where the light He speaks of is not that of the sun but only of a candle, there is a glad, triumphant tone: "If thy whole body be full of light, having no part dark, the whole shall be full of light, as when the bright shining of a candle doth give thee light." He fondles His image, and holds on to it, and turns it over and over as if loth to part with it—a natural feeling, for it stood for all He taught and was; He Himself was the Light of the world. See this clearly with a true and honest eye; look straight and full upon it; blow away the blinding mists; open your eyes wide, and this light will fill you; and even as the world does all its work by reason of light, so you will have light, and enough of it, for all you have to do.

Something like this, I suppose, is the meaning; but it is altogether too great a meaning for a sermon, being well-nigh the whole Gospel, and so I will speak of a certain side of it, or rather of a suggestion it starts, which I will name as the illuminating power of a supreme principle.

It is a constantly recurring question—how to secure character. By character I mean a full development of our nature. Sift all other theories of character—culture, happiness, achievement—and while they have weight and carry one a long way, they run out at last, and lose meaning, simply because they are within finite limits. The time comes to every man, and to all men taken together, when culture, happiness, achievement cease to have meaning, for they have passed beyond their spheres. The only conceivable thing that can be named as the object or end of life is *character*, for the simple reason that it is the only thing that lasts. In other words, the only rational object we can set before us is to take this self made up of mind and heart and will, and train it in the line of its creative design, bring out all its powers, train it away from its faults and defects, make it strong and compact and substantial—a real thing, harmonious, true, the very thing it was designed to be. Then we have something that lasts, something that does not dissolve under the touch of time and death.

There is no reason to hope for

anything permanent except as we fall in with God's creative plans. Then we move along with God, and on His lines of action and purpose. If character is God's purpose in creating me I must fall in with this purpose, or reap certain failure. Along that one line and towards that one end I must strive and win, or be left a castaway on the shores of Eternity.

So much is plain to the simplest: fall into God's plan or fail. Who cannot understand that? Now, the attainment of character may have other names; it may be clothed in many ways; it will run along many lines. You may call it *heaven* if you will think of heaven as perfected character—character come to its full in the presence of God. You may call it *salvation*, if you mean that in this race of life in which we are running towards the goal of character we escape its inevitable dangers. You may call it *redemption*, if you mean that in the production of character we must, as it were, be redeemed—bought off—from the forces of nature, the low and brutish conditions in which we find ourselves, the world of appetite and native selfishness, in order to clear and free this self, this soul that we are, from its entanglements before we can well begin to train and develop it. There is so much of this to do that I know of no term that so well covers the process as redemption, and I like to think of myself as a redeemed being, and of the world as a redeemed world—that is, brought out of lower conditions into higher, and always at the cost of suffering, for in no other way can the higher be drawn out of the lower. But when we say *redemption* we do not mean an act or process that stops with itself. We are not redeemed into heaven and future glory; we are redeemed out of evil; and then begins the real business of life. Redemption simply clears the field for action, and makes it ready for character to lay its foundations and build itself up. Or you may call it *service*, doing one's work, and filling one's place in the world—a very noble and imperative conception of life; but do you not see that all this service, all this doing and striving, contemplates some end or result? Else, you turn the world into a vain round. Some day the service stops, and what then? It passes over into the next generation, it is said. Well, but the next generation ends, and at last all the generations end, and then what has become of the service? Like the players' revels, it has "dissolved into thin air." Unless the service has transmuted itself into character, it is swept out upon the unreturning tide of time, and is gone for ever.

But it is the blessed thing about *service*, this common task of us all, that it can be transmuted into character. Service is the stuff out of which character is made. That which all *must* do is made the basis of that which all should achieve. Service means fidelity, and fidelity means character, and character is an abiding and eternal finality. And when the service takes on devotion and sacrifice and love, then it creates a character which not only endures, but shines with the very glory of God.

Thus you see that the one thing we have to do is to strive after character; to take this self and make it what God meant it should be. And let me say to those who are, or expect to become teachers of religion, that any theory of duty or service, or of man's relation to God, any doctrine of the atonement or of salvation, that does not turn on and end in character is not only worthless, but false. The universe is a moral universe, and character is its sole product.

As I have intimated, it is character in its large sense, not character in a legal nor in a conventional sense, but character as the fulfilment of our nature—the unfolding of all our powers, the perfect being made in the image of God, perfecting and bringing out the image—this is the character of which we are speaking. Under such a conception, it becomes the question of questions how best to secure character; how to start and foster its growth; how to guard it from its enemies and keep it on right lines; how to supply it with motive power; how to enrich and ennoble it; how to carry it along from one period of life to another, so that it shall not stop by the way; how to keep it steadily under the great inspirations which God is breathing upon it, and by which it is made divine, and shaped into the divine likeness—questions that comprise well-nigh the whole business of life.

I can touch the subject only at

one or two points. Character is often spoken of as a certain condition, essential to safety and respectability, into which one can be trained by a drill of rules and habits. Perhaps the commonest conception of it is that it can be secured by paying attention to the details of conduct and by the formation of good habits. A man of character is often regarded as one who is irreproachable in these respects. Now, such a man is so useful, and is so much above the average, that it is not best to find fault with him, nor is fault to be found with him. It is not what he *is* that is to be criticised, but what he is *not*. It would be a mistake to let such a man stand as an example of that great thing which embraces all our powers and determines our destiny. Besides, we are not dealing with sources and means of power, nor are we on the road to great results, when we are dealing with details of conduct, and with what are called good habits. They are of great value, but they may be over-valued. We cannot go one step in education without insisting on them. It is a large part of education at home and in school to form them. They are imperatively necessary. The discipline to mind and body in securing them is all-essential; and when acquired they become a part of the machinery of life; they act automatically, and save continuous efforts of the will; they preserve unity of effort and keep one on a straight path; they conserve energy and carry a man onward almost without his own will. By all means let us have good habits and take all possible pains to teach them. They are tools to work with; they are carriages to ride in; they are servants to work for us; but just because they are these they cannot assume the control of us and mould our destiny. Thank God for every good habit you have learned. The learning it did you much good, and the use of it is a constant help. It is like capital in business—something to fall back on. But just as capital does not take the place of the commercial spirit, so a good habit does not take the place of a constant play of the moral nature. Indeed, there comes a time when habit ceases to be moral. As it becomes fixed and automatic the moral passes out of it, and it becomes necessary. It is none the less useful in the everyday work of life; but it ceases to enrich and feed the soul. One who has so formed the habit of industry that he is unhappy when not at work is fortunate; but his habit is doing nothing for him morally. In that respect he has passed out of the world of freedom, where alone there is morality, into the world of necessity, where there is no morality. Evolution and the new psychology have taught us that man has been brought out of necessity and instinct, which is but fixed habit, into a world of freedom. To be a man is to be free; to be a brute is to be under necessity. But we cannot all at once become free; freedom is too great and fine a thing to have at first. To be wholly free is to be spirit; for only a spirit has full freedom. While we are on the way to become spirits, we must carry along with us something of the necessity out of which we came. Wordsworth says that "trailing clouds of glory do we come from God who is our home." True, for God is the home of all created things; but it is also true that we come out of the depths of nature, trailing clouds of brutish instinct and necessity, conditions needful to us. They uphold us, and contain us while the wings of our spirit are growing into readiness for flight into the world of utter freedom.

Now, habit is a wise use of the

necessity of lower nature; it corresponds to instinct in the brutes. Life would be unendurable, it could not go on, it would wear itself out and work in random ways and to no purpose, if we were forced to make fresh choices whenever we needed to act. And so we go back into that primeval world, which is also God's world, and we say to it: Lend us your law of necessity to use while we are achieving our freedom; lend us something as near instinct as possible, so that we may not be crushed under our great gift of freedom.

Such is the place of habit in relation to character—of unspeakable value in creating the framework and doing the everyday work of life; but habit is not character. No combination of good habits would constitute character; nor do they go beyond a certain point in feeding and shaping character.

What, then, is it that does this? Here, I think, the text helps us.

The man does not light himself; nor does he light a few tapers of good habits on one side and some candles of wise maxims on another side; he does not carry a lamp of virtue in his hand, and so pick out a safe path. All this is very well. I like the moralists, and am willing that Marcus Aurelius should be canonised as a saint; but as furnishing a solution of our nature and meeting its necessities they are insufficient. They lack vital force.

Christ spake in precepts, but He is all the while transcending them and rising into higher conceptions of life and destiny—as here. Open your eyes — having made them clear and true—and light, not your light nor any light of earth, but light from above—will shine through them and fill your whole body.

Christ was constantly putting men into relation to the unseen and eternal world. He was always opening the heavens and beholding what was there. Out of heaven came the motives and the inspirations with which He constantly plied men. The moving and shaping powers were there.

All this teaching may be summed up as an effort to bring us under inspirations and forces that are commensurate with our nature. Christ gave us something that was large enough for us; something strong enough to command us; something glorious enough to win us; something wide enough to cover our whole nature, and to last us for ever. He passed by all the petty rules and details of conduct, and gave us a few great principles to go by. He passed by all our superficial tastes and likings, and touched our nature in its depths—conscience and love and reverence. He did not concern Himself with the details of government and social procedure, but held up the kingdom of God, with its few simple requirements of justice and humanity and righteousness. He said little or nothing about time or death, nothing about the vanity of one nor the sadness of the other, but lifted us above them into another world—a world of reality, of constant fulfilment, where the real process of our life is for ever going on.

It is the revelation of this that constituted Christ's work; and He made us feel it because He felt it Himself. It was an absolute reality to Him. He saw God, and knew that He was the Father. He looked at the world and through it, and saw a spiritual world behind it; and this world was man's world. To bring men under its power was the purpose and struggle of His life. The secret of His success lay in this—that when He thus uncovered the spiritual world and revealed its powers, He aroused in men all the real passion of their nature;

passion, I say, for that is the central thing in man—the ability to feel and to respond to motives for action; to feel—that is, to cast one's self with all one's powers into a cause or purpose which one approves—this is the grand and central characteristic of man.

Now, it is easy enough to interest men in one thing and another. Man is a many-sided and responsive being, yielding quickly to any call made to him, easily aroused to enthusiasm. But there are only a few things that call out this central passion. Art, perhaps, will do it, for there is something divine in art. Love certainly will do it, for love is essentially divine. But all this busy play of human life, its strifes and labours, do not represent the deepest feelings of man. They have their day and end. There is nothing that arouses the real passion of his nature but that which is commensurate with his nature. We respond superficially to slight motives; we are easily pleased. But you do not really move us until you touch the fundamental and essential parts of our nature. Only deep responds to deep. It is only as the waters are made according to gravitation that they respond to it, and they respond because they are so made, and thus become the ceaseless tide that for ever obeys the heavenly attraction. The waters rise and fall in waves as the winds touch them; there are strong and steady currents flowing here and there; they break on rocky shores and lose themselves on sandy beaches—all this, but the one permanent motion that takes up and outmasters all the others is the heaven-drawn tide. It is so with man. It is only eternal things that deeply and permanently move him; for he was made for them. And so, when Christ uncovers these eternal things, we surrender to them and pour out upon them all the passion of our nature, and give ourselves up to them.

And thus there begins this moulding process; then character begins to take shape, to strike its roots into the eternal verities and to gather colour and lustre in their light; it grows from above, because there it finds what will feed it.

The passion for God never dies out, and it never ceases to mould one into the image of God. The passion for righteousness never ceases to move a man when it has once laid hold of him. See how relentless and implacable it is to-day as it stands before the betrayals of trusts and the corruptions of justice. And it never gives over imparting itself to him who loves it; for more and more does one see and feel that one was made after its pattern. The passion for humanity, once awakened, never dies out; for we not only more and more feel the eternal rightness and fitness of it, but the satisfaction of it grows continually deeper and sweeter. One who has once conceived a true passion for humanity will be for ever consumed with it; and it will also for ever transform and mould one into the likeness of Him who was humanity itself. As these great facts and verities wrap themselves around a man, and enter into him, and mingle with his feelings do they give shape and colour to him, and become absolutely character; for they are moulding him according to his nature, and for his destiny.

The subject is very near and practical. I do not think there is less sense of the worth of character now than in the past; I do not know but our ways of securing it are, upon the whole, as good as those of the past. But, comparisons aside, it is easy to see that poor and inadequate means are much used and depended upon to secure it. It is sought in a multiplicity of ways, and most of them are small ways. We depend upon a drill in good habits, upon companionship, upon education, upon refined tastes, upon home influence, upon safe environment—all good, but insufficient. They do not cover and command our nature; they are not strong enough to create a permanent tendency and movement in the young mind. Alongside of these good influences are the tremendous forces of the human heart that require something as great as itself to shape and direct it. We often say with Augustine: "Thou, O God, hast made us for Thyself, and our hearts are restless till they rest in Thee." It is true, but there is something truer than that; because God has made us for Himself and like Himself; He alone can lead and mould our nature into that likeness. In God only can you find motives strong enough to move one made in His image. The feelings and ideas and passions that unite to shape us and to lead us towards our destiny, must spring out of God, and come to us as from God.

Hence our supreme and constant effort should be to keep ourselves and our children under the power of religion; and let us see to it that it is religion and not some faint image of it; *religion—* the knowledge of God, the fear of God, the love of God, the worship of God, the service of God, and all that play of heart and spirit that these things imply.

Thus, and thus only, can we win character strong enough for the work of life, and substantial enough to endure when life is over.

Rest through Humility.

> Come unto Me, all ye that labour and are heavy laden, and I will give you rest. Take My yoke upon you, and learn of Me; for I am meek and lowly in heart; and ye shall find rest unto your souls. For My yoke is easy, and My burden is light.
> St. Matt. xi. 28, 29, 30.

WE are apt to use these words as we do music, which is for feeling and not for thought. The feeling is so much more prominent than the thought, and it so readily allies itself with our own feelings that we get no farther, and the gracious words of our Lord fall on us like strains of music that soothe and comfort by a charm of their own, but make no appeal to the reason. I do not deny that this is a proper use of them; for as there are times when only music can reach the trouble and unrest of our spirits, so, in like seasons, the soothing tenderness and repose of these words are all that we need, all that we can endure.

But I venture to believe that Christ had in mind, not merely nor chiefly the extreme sufferings of humanity, but also the commoner forms, the universal weariness and unrest that in one way or another beset us all. Extreme sorrow needs only comfort and sympathy, a friend and helper upon whom it can simply pour itself out, but the calmer yet not less real unrest that is the common lot, can be met by reason; that is, it can examine the method by which Christ gives us rest, and knowing the method, the mind as well as the spirit will move toward the helping Christ.

Let us try to detach the text from its associations as a mere voice of consolation, and look at it with the careful eye of analysis; perhaps it may thus have more power to comfort; at least we shall learn how it is that Christ gives rest to the weary and heavy laden.

1. It is a process of learning.

Christ's gift of rest is not dropped all at once and without means into the soul, but is something *learned*, and therefore is gained by a process. But it is no less a gift because we ourselves must work to secure it. We ask God to give us our daily bread and go directly forth to earn it, full of faith still that it is given in answer to our prayer. So in this matter of *rest*, though we are not apt to think of it in the same way, because bread is a thing and rest is a feeling. This word *learn* is generally overlooked, and we turn to Christ expecting that by some spiritual miracle a sudden peace will be created within us. I do not deny but there may be crises of trouble and spiritual suffering when an impression of immediate peace is granted, but it is not lasting. It may remain as a precious memory, but we soon sink back to our ordinary level. We did not thus establish a law and an order of peace in our hearts; that must come by the slower process of learning. Nothing can get permanent lodgment within us in any other way. That which comes in suddenly goes out suddenly. That which is born of impulse dies with the impulse. It is not God's plan that character should be made up by out-and-out gifts, but that it should *grow*—He Himself feeding its springs and directing its progress.

All this applies with special force to finding rest from the labours and heavy burdens of life. Christ does not take them off at once, He works no spiritual miracle by which the cares of life are dispelled; there is no exorcising as by magic. He says, instead, "Take My yoke upon you, and *learn* of Me." He evidently has chiefly in mind, not acute cases of suffering, nor those who are overwhelmed by sudden catastrophe. I hesitate to say this, lest it may seem to take this great word of comfort away from those who are suffering in extreme ways. Let these remember that Scripture is full of promises suited more directly to their case. Instead, our Lord has in mind the vast multitudes who are weary and sick at heart because of unsatisfied desires, who hopelessly long for what they never can get, and those who repine because their selfish claims and fancied deserts are not paid at the counter of the world. He sees that the great majority of men are ill at ease, unsatisfied, wretched, and so He says to them: You are living in a false way; you have taken upon your necks the heavy yoke of the world, the yoke of pride and ambition and selfishness; it is crushing you, taking all the joy out of your lives, chafing and harassing you by its fruitless weight; leave the world, where such burdens originate, and come unto Me; throw off its heavy burdens and take My easy yoke upon you and learn of Me; I will teach you a better way to live, and will so lead you into rest.

2. What is the process that Christ has in mind?

There must first be a reception of Christ Himself as the Divine Master of Men. His method of helping and saving men is personal; He is a real Saviour in a real world; He is more than thought to thinking men—He is life to living men. Hence, a man cannot be saved — saved from himself, from his weakness, from his unrest, until he comes into this personal and immediate relation to Christ as Lord and Master. The men of science tell us that the world is not only a revelation of the will of God, but that it is itself the will of God. So Christ is not only a teacher of truth, but is the truth itself. When a man lives in the world, obeying its laws, he lives in and through the will of God. So one must live in and through Christ in order to get at the power of His truth. This world is a real world, and nothing can be won from it except by real processes.

This brings us to the question: How is it that, by learning of Christ, we are rid of the wearying burdens of life, and find rest to our souls? The answer is at hand:—by learning of Christ in those forms or qualities in which He offers Himself—*meekness* and *lowliness* of heart. Learn of Me, for I am meek and lowly of heart, and ye shall find rest to your souls. He does not say—learn of Me because I am wise, or merciful, or benevolent; instead, He says that rest is the outcome of *meekness* and *humility*, and that the labours and heavy burdens of life spring from pride and self-assertion. I doubt if ever a plummet dropped deeper into human nature than this; and yet how plain it is that by far the greater part of the painful restlessness and weariness and burden-bearing from which we suffer, springs from our pride and self-assertion. I do not forget the anguish of death, the ravages of vice, the horrors of crime. More than these, because it is closer and more constant, is the painful unrest of the human heart as it proudly strives after that which it does not deserve. Ruskin says that "Vanity after Pride is the most fatal of all sins, fretting the whole depth of our humanity into storm." If we were each one to get down to the source of our own unrest, our cloudiness of spirit, our inward complaining, should we not find that they are due to some selfish or vain desire, some eager ambition, some claim that the world does not see fit to honour, some selfish expectation that fails of gratification, some undue assertion of self?

A deeper vanity is meant than that which goes under its commonly recognised trappings. It is this thrusting forward of self in its numberless forms to which Christ offsets a meek and lowly heart; this setting up of self as the centre and the main thing to be considered. Now this is not simply wrong; that feature of it is waived by Christ in the text; it is wretched and miserable and makes life a burden, for there is no load a man carries so heavy as self.

The keen pitying eye of Christ fixed at once upon this source of human misery, and He singled it out from the pains of the body and the griefs of the heart, that He might bestow upon it His tenderest compassion and heal it with the surest remedy. And the remedy, of course, must lie in a substitution of the opposite quality —a meek and lowly mind.

See how this works. Humility may be roughly defined as the putting away or forgetting of self. I know that it will be said that this is not the way to get on in the world; but there is something better than getting *on* in the world, and that is, getting *above* the world. There is a lower success that is earned through proud and vigorous self-assertion, and its reward is the unrest of a being made for better things. There is a success that comes from losing the life, from curbing self with perpetual meekness, from walking in ways of humility and self-denial, and its reward is *rest*—the rest of unimpeded energies working for ever in the line of their true destiny.

The method and working of humility are seldom well understood. It is a blind grace, hard to define, hard to put into a clear form; and, above all, it is liable to perversion. It is often treated as a spiritless quality, as allied to passiveness and inefficiency, as opposed to alertness and self-reliance, and the aggressiveness of strong and vigorous life; and as such it is caricatured in literature and common speech. Hence it needs to be carefully defined and conceived. As I think of it, it is the reverse of all this. It is at root a disenthralment of self, a clearing of the mind from all hindrances so that it enters the arena of life free and unhindered for its battles. There is no impediment in the path of life so great as self. There is nothing that so ties the hands and feet in great and noble enterprises as a proud consciousness of self. The man who truly wins is he who sees an end and looks on himself simply as a force for gaining it— himself as something to be used as a means, not as an end.

There is such a thing as a *high* humility, a *noble* humility, a *brave* humility. Humility is not the negation of personality; it is not a reduction of self-hood to nothingness, but rather a refusal to erect self into a governing motive; it is personality utterly devoted to a cause—self at work, but self forgotten while at work.

We must not forget that we are to learn this from Christ, not merely by word of mouth, but by going to Him and following Him. He was meek and lowly in heart, and *therefore* had rest in His soul; not rest outwardly—that He promises to none—but rest within. Pride had no foothold in His life, and so His peace was perfect. Retaining His lowly condition when all the kingdoms of the earth were offered Him, meek when falsely persecuted, doing the will of the Father with simple fidelity while all the world scoffed, crucified at last because He would not save Himself, He carried all the while a heaven of rest in His soul. And to such fellowship He summons us. "Take My yoke upon you and learn of Me; *for I am meek and lowly of heart, and ye shall find rest unto your souls.*"

Nearness the Secret of Power.

> But the righteousness which is of faith saith thus, Say not in thy heart, Who shall ascend into heaven? (That is, to bring Christ down:) or, Who shall descend into the abyss? (That is, to bring Christ up from the dead.) But what saith it? The word is nigh thee, in thy mouth, and in thy heart: that is, the word of faith, which we preach.—ROMANS x. 6-8.

THERE is one thing, among many others, that St. Paul did for religion—he made it a *near* matter. There is no need of going up into the heavens nor down into the depths to realise its power; it is a near thing—this word of faith, this Christly energy, this saving hope.

Here we touch a universal law, namely, the condition of all power is nearness. Whether in lifting a weight or exerting an influence, you must be near the thing you are engaged upon. Gravitation itself almost loses its hold through distance, decreasing by rapid ratio as it crosses the void of space, and increasing as the attracting bodies approach each other. Granite is solid because its atoms lie close to one another.

The same is true of religion and morals and education. If in either field you desire to exert or to feel an influence the power must be near.

It is said by those who are wise in the new science of pedagogy that the deepest and most formative lessons received by the human mind are those conveyed by the loving touch and caress of the mother upon the child before it has come to a consciousness of itself. It is sufficiently wonderful and gracious that the first impressions and lessons should be those of pure love, but it is even more wonderful that they should be conveyed by touch alone, and before the object of them has begun to think, or to know itself. Do we not even thus lie in the embrace of God, and feel, though we know it not, the touch of His love?

This is the struggle of religion —to get and to keep near to men. When God is distant, men do not feel Him. Hence, all religions appear in the form of revelations —a drawing nigh to men. In vain are men asked to believe in a God afar off. He must at least come as near as some mountain-top or mystic cave, whence He can speak in thunder or whisper in oracles. So, when a religion becomes old, and the facts on which it depends grow remote, it loses power. The distance of time is as fatal to influence as the distance of space. Hence the complaint and protest heard on all sides against the preaching of remote facts in Hebrew history; and the criticism is just, unless these facts can in some way be transformed into present realities. This is the reason why new religions are all the while springing up, and why men are constantly modifying old religions, making them over like a garment, so that they will present a new appearance, and offer new attractions. Religion must be kept near, a ready and close-at-hand matter, and the religion that best succeeds in doing this—if it keeps within the lines of truth—will have the most power. In the long run, it is not ancient truths and facts that most move men, but the truth and fact of to-day—a divinely wise arrangement, for if it were not so there would be no progress. The attempt to rehabilitate religion with its ancient forms is and ought to be a failure.

Now, Christianity is such a religion—near, present, fresh, close at hand. It is not a *fixed* religion, for ever chanting an ancient creed, but an ever-developing religion, adapting itself to each new generation. If any crisis comes in the world's history, Christianity stands ready to meet it with some healing remedy or some guiding principle. Just as fast as the world outgrows or overthrows its social forms, Christianity comes forward with others to take their place. So liberty and justice and humanity fill the place of tyranny and slavery, until there comes to be even a Christian civilisation and a Christian nation. Nor is there any end to this process, this fresh and constant insertion of itself into the upheavals of society and becoming to it a law and guide. It has an affinity for society, and for man in all his troubles. Whenever questions of great moment arise, like those which mark English and American history, Christianity comes to the front and stands by, deciding who shall govern, who shall be free, who shall be educated, how crime shall be punished, what spirit shall enter into legislation, what principle shall decide doubtful questions.

The secret and power of Christianity do not consist in a historical unity running back into ancient facts, but in the fact of present power by which it can throw itself into the questions of to-day and determine their settlement. And Christ is no Christ except as He walks in the Western Continent even as He walked in Galilee; He is no Saviour except as He dies to-day in the sacrifices of His followers.

This fact of nearness as the condition of power has a good illustration in the ideas of God which have prevailed.

There is no doubt but that the discoveries of modern astronomy have weakened the sense of God; or, if not weakened, have thrown it into confusion. One reason why the Hebrew believed that God took so great a part in personal and national affairs was that his world was small; it was not too much for God to regulate; He could supervise a man's life down to his going out and his coming in. God was near and was adequate to meet every detail of need or conduct. But when all this began to change under the discoveries of science, and the world shrank to its little place, and the heavens began to spread out into infinity, God receded into them and became lost to this world in the countless multitudes that were brought into view. Hence it became more and more difficult for faith to believe that God interested Himself in human affairs. The great facts of personal inspiration and communion with God, individual care, and finally the doctrine of Christ as the incarnation of God grew weak. Nor could the breach in faith be healed by the metaphysical idea that, as God is infinite, He can cover an infinite universe—true as logic and true in fact, but who *feels* it? It is still difficult to realise that the Lord of endless worlds is the Lord of our personal lives, and so we lapse into the thought that they are ordered by *laws*; and when law is put in place of the direct action of God, it is all over with faith; if all is of law and there is no God, there is no use in trying to believe anything.

This waning and evaporating of the conception of God is not on the decrease. As the telescopes broaden their lenses, and with every increased inch of aperture deepen the universe by immeasurable millions of miles, so faith grows proportionately weak and thin. The old saying, that "the undevout astronomer is mad," loses its force; not devout nor mad, but confused or agnostic; and we all tend to think with him.

Plainly there must be another conception of God, if we are to have a God. Have a God men will in the long run. Only for a season will they be content to leave themselves and the worlds without cause or explanation. And this can never be found so long as we look for God outside of creation. Reverse this conception; put God inside of His works instead of outside of them; think not of Him as an external directing power, but as an indwelling force and life; think that He is the law itself, and the life of any creature is God's life, that any force which acts is the force of God—think in these ways, and you will once more find God near you, and the thought of Him will warm your soul into new life and feed it with its congenial food. No matter now how wide the Lick telescope expands "the flaming walls of the world"; we no longer ascend into the heavens to bring

God down, nor descend into the abysmal depths of space and time to bring Him up; He is not there, or He is there only in some phenomenal sense; His real presence is *within* His creation, and His *full* presence is where there is a consciousness of Him as *within*.

This conception was fundamental to Christ. He used only the inward eye, and even when He looked without it was still with inward vision. The world was never so full of God and so visible as when He closed His eyes in prayer at night in the dark recesses of mountain gorges. Over and over again He said that the kingdom of heaven was at hand; it was nigh; it was within. The revelation is not from without by flesh and blood, by creational forms, but *within*, and by the Father Himself. The one struggle of Christ was to break up externalism and all the outward searches after God, and to get men to look within themselves, to search their own hearts, when they can find Him for the simple reason that He is there.

The discoveries of science are of immense value, but they do not of themselves help one very much in one's search after God. One who is using them is looking in the wrong direction; he is not looking through the wrong end of the telescope; he is using the wrong kind of glass; he needs a mirror, one that will show himself and all his inward being. In himself, in the wonder of his nature, in the play of his powers, in his wants and needs and longings and aspirations he will find God, because he is made in the image of God. The external world is not the image of God, but merely an unformed or forming image that as yet reveals nothing very clearly. Nature is only, as Novalis said, "an illuminated table of the contents of the Spirit"—not the book itself.

This effort and purpose of Christ are an explanation of what seem defects in Him, and what seems a lack of practicality; no Church for which He seemed to care, no Bible, no drill in observances, no organisation, no creed—all useful things that inevitably came about and inevitably will continue; Bible and Church, and drill and organisation and creed we must have, but Christ waived them for the time in order to drive men in upon themselves, and to get them to search their own natures, where alone they could find their God and Father. The method is not different to-day. Church and Bible and drill and creed we need and must have, but the real business is within; there is where we find God, there we feel His truth and grace and power, if anywhere. St. Paul, by one brief word, told the truth in regard to the whole matter: " It pleased God to reveal His Son *in* me," not *to*, but *in*. It is *within* that the revelations of God are made, and Christ is not a revelation even as He hangs upon the cross until He has been brought into the inner world where faith and love and spiritual vision lay hold of Him. He is too far off when He hangs upon the cross on distant Calvary; too far off if put at the end of the twenty centuries. He must be with us always. He must become as daily bread that we eat, and so mix His being with ours. He must become as wine that we drink, and thus mingle His very life-blood with our own.

It is all, you see, a matter of nearness. That word *near* is wellnigh the whole secret of religion; it is certainly the secret of its power. Draw nigh to God and He will draw nigh to you; only we must see to it that it is a real drawing nigh, and not an approach with words. Often we must clear away impeding sins, and climb over great masses of indifference, and break through closed doors of selfish habits, and scale precipices of dulness and sloth before we can get at God, or, rather, before God can get at us. God can do nothing for us; He cannot teach, nor comfort, nor inspire, nor strengthen us: He cannot lift us out of this perishing world until He and the souls we are come face to face— He breathing upon us with His living breath, laying hold of us with His strong, pitying hands; and we in like manner pressing close to Him, our hearts longing after Him, our spirits resting in Him, our wills obedient to Him, and our whole being throwing itself with conscious sympathy into the current of His plans and works.

Our Lord, in the last supper with the disciples, had come into the full consciousness that He was One with the Father. He did not have this consciousness on the ground of identity of being or nature—that was an inference—but on the ground of His having come into the mid-stream of God's ways and will. He had said with full meaning and purpose, " Not My will but Thine be done." He had climbed to the summit of the eternal truth that God is Love, and that love works by sacrifice. He saw that the way of life, for Him and for all, was to cast Himself joyfully into the current of God's will and to let it sweep Him wherever it would, even through the gulfs of death. By thus losing His life, He knew He should find it; by dying in the hands of God, He knew that He was entering into the fulness of life.

The sacrament of the supper sets forth Christ at the height of His career, and that height meant oneness with the Father. Faith and obedience and patience and humility had done their work, and

He rested in the full consciousness of oneness with God. The peace of God possessed Him. His joy was full, for He had entered into the secret of God, and knew the Eternal from the beginning, even the love which was from the beginning.

It was out of such a consciousness that this service of remembrance sprang—*an achieved oneness with the Father.*

While it was at its fullest and intensest, He sought to impart it to His disciples so that they might share it, or at least learn the way into it. And so He said, "Remember Me as I am now—this oneness with the Father, this peace and joy; remember how I came into it—by obedience and trust, even to the laying down of My life."

Let us assure ourselves what this rite means and says. Its purpose is not to fix our gaze upon the bloody tragedy of Calvary. It does more than repeat a great example of love and fidelity. It does not mean expiation—penal suffering and satisfied justice. It is rather an invitation to draw nigh to Christ and share His life when it was at its highest point; not the suffering of it, but the joy and peace of it when it had gone through the toil and struggle and temptation, and had reached the point when He could say, "I and My Father are one"; My will is His will; My love is His love. Through faith and patience and obedience I have learned the secret of God and found it to be blessedness.

Such is the feast which we share with Christ; we feed our souls upon Him even as we feed our bodies upon bread and wine; we unite ourselves with an eternal Person in whom we find the realisation of our own highest thoughts and purposes, and whatever else is good and true.

How to Live in the World.

> For the grace of God hath appeared, bringing salvation to all men, instructing us to the intent that, denying ungodliness and worldly lusts, we should live soberly and righteously and godly in this present world.
> TITUS II. 11, 12.

THIS epistle is made up of two parts: one telling what sort of a man a bishop or minister should be, the other what he should teach. It is intensely practical, but the injunctions rest on spiritual truths, and presuppose a spiritual life. St. Paul always had a tremendous reason for the simplest duty; his motives are always great and far-reaching. This is not only Pauline, but Christian—great reasons for doing little things; high motives for all conduct; every act linked to some eternal purpose—this is the distinctive feature of Christianity. It appears in the text. He would have Titus teach the Cretans to be sober and righteous and godly, but he prefaces it by a statement of the great *Gospel*—a word which is itself full of beauty, a sweet, melodious word: "For the grace of God hath appeared, bringing salvation to all men." It sounds like a strain caught from an angel's hymn. It is that, and it is also solid truth. All Christian injunctions and precepts rest on that truth—God's grace appearing and bringing salvation to all men. That fact is the ground on which we stand; it is the atmosphere about us; it is motive, path, end. God's gracious love, not sought or deduced, but appearing by its own spontaneous will, moved by its own yearning heart, bringing salvation to all men, so that it is here, an already accomplished fact, food to eat, air to breathe, shelter to cover us—a great investing fact or condition, changing our whole life and giving direction to it. It is such a truth that St. Paul puts under his advice, expecting that the advice would get its force and clinch from the truth. He has nothing to say about life or duty except upon the basis of this truth. All else is night and darkness; this is day and light. While we keep in mind that we are living in a world overspread by the love of God, working for the salvation of all men; when we understand that that is the kind of world we are in, then we are ready to give shape to conduct and to take up our duties. This fact makes the climate of the world; it redeems it from the hard severity of external nature, and makes it warm and genial and productive; it plants in its soil hope and cheer and confidence. It is all-important to understand what sort of a world we are in; then we have ground and reason for action, and inspiration to secure it.

This being understood, St. Paul goes on to tell us how we should live. That is the question of questions—how to live in this world—with what spirit, and for what end. It is not so simple a matter as it seems, nor are men agreed upon it. It is the question that earnest minds are all the while asking; it underlies education; parents ask it anxiously for their children; every young man comes to a parting of the ways, when he asks what path he shall take. There are vast numbers who do not know how to live in the world. It is one of the mysteries of human life that we should not know how to live it. It is the strange and pathetic thing about life that it is all we have to do, and we do not know how to do it.

I think we come as near finding a true plan of living in these words as can be found anywhere—

"denying ungodliness and worldly lusts, we should live soberly, righteously, and godly in this present world."

Much is being said now in regard to different types of Christianity—an Oriental type and an Occidental type, a first-century type, a mediæval type, and a modern type; and we also hear of a possible Japanese type and Hindu type. There is some truth in such distinctions, but, after all, there is but one type of true life. No matter when a man lived, there was but one way to live—a sober, righteous, and godly way. No matter what type of Christian life may be developed in Japan or India, it must be a sober, righteous, and godly type.

These words are both general and definite; they are like the Arab's tent which could be clasped by his hand or spread wide enough to shelter his whole tribe.

Take the first word—"soberly."

It is perhaps not the best for conveying the writer's idea. It is now used chiefly to describe demeanour; by a sober person we mean one of staid and sedate behaviour. But the thought goes deeper. Three other words taken together convey its sense—*sanely, intelligently, earnestly;* they are all wrapped up in the original word. To live soberly is to live sanely—that is, according to the laws of our nature; intelligently—that is, with open eyes, taking account of methods and means ans consequences, using our faculties aright and for right ends; earnestly—how better can it be defined than by itself?—*earnestly*, taking life as a reality and not as a jest, a time for work and not for play, for achievement and not for pleasure; holding life as something to be deeply considered and set to a use; as something into which one is to throw one's self with all one's powers as having inexpressible worth and dignity, and to be lived accordingly; such is its meaning. It is the first requisite in life that we shall be earnest. It is the quality that wise parents and teachers most desire to awaken in their children and pupils. If they can see signs of earnestness they feel sure that all will be well. An earnest young man almost never makes a failure of life; one without earnestness can make of life nothing but failure; the lack of it is itself failure. I do not mean that earnestness will surely yield a good life, but rather that it starts one in right directions; it sets one in motion, and the movement is generally towards what is good. For a young man seldom cherishes ignoble purposes; the heart of youth is set to things high and true. If he is ambitious there is a halo about his dream. It is only in rare cases that he deliberately resolves to live for himself, and to win a selfish success. Nearly always he would do good, and help others, and serve his age and country—dreams often shattered in the after-conflicts of life, but they are the materials put within us out of which life is to be built. When they are taken up by a true earnestness they grow into abiding realities. How parents long to see the signs of it in their children. How closely the father watches the face and tones of his boy to catch the first signs of solid purpose and real thought of life. How eagerly a mother looks into the heart of her daughter for the signs of a true womanhood. Wise teachers care less for the way the lessons are learned or not learned than for a certain spirit of earnestness and real purpose to be found in a boy, if it is in him; if they can see that they have hope of him whether he recites well or ill. Hence many a boy is kept in school or college by his teachers because of earnestness in some one department of study, though careless in others. For his success does not depend upon having learned a certain number of good lessons, but upon an earnest purpose to do some special thing that is worthy of effort. The lessons will be forgotten; the purpose will abide, for it belongs to the man himself.

It is one of the great services rendered by Dr. Arnold, of Rugby, that he substituted the word *earnest* for *serious*, not because the words are in themselves very different in meaning, but because *serious* had come to stand for a type of character which he did not like—studiously careful demeanour, repression of feelings, unnatural gravity, in short, the marks of the piety of the aged adopted in youth. All this was repulsive to him; for, as Bishop Phillips Brooks once told the students at Harvard, "the main feature in Christian life is *naturalness*." It is not natural for a young man to be serious, but it is natural for him to be earnest. It is the quality that Dr. Arnold strove to awaken and keep alive in his pupils, and with such success that he trained for England a generation of men such as no other age or nation has produced.

Earnestness is at first an intense desire to do something, to achieve results, to make a name, or to win a place. Of course, it plays about self, and wears the form of ambition; but no matter for that, it must be so at first. But under education it begins to take shape and direction. It passes into the will, and so becomes the life-blood of a calling. It enters into the conscience, and makes one the faithful servant of one's age and country. It enters into one's religion, and turns it into unconquerable purpose and unwearying fidelity.

But life must also be *righteous*. Soberness refers to the hidden temper or spirit of one's life; it is wholly personal, but this refers to one's relation to others. *Live in right relations to your fellowmen* is what the text says. But is this specially Christian? Do not all men and all religions say the same? Yes, but not quite in the same way, nor with the same scope of meaning. The writer of the epistle says it upon the background of his previous word— "For the grace of God hath appeared, bringing salvation to all men." He urged nothing, as I have said, except upon the basis of the Gospel. He thus carried the truth or duty into the eternal world of reality, where it got meaning, and sanction, and purpose, and end. That is, he planted all duty upon God, and allied it to God's action. He says that the grace of God is here in the world, saving men by teaching them to love and serve and pity and help one another; the grace of God must become the grace of every man—each one repeating that grace in his own life; it is upon *such* a background that he tells us to live a righteous life.

This is something far more than observance of the common maxims of honesty and fairness and justice; it is righteousness, with God behind it, and with God's very process of gracious love and righteousness going on around us. It makes a great difference whether we live a righteous life out of a sense of *this* world, or out of a sense of the *eternal* world; because the laws require it, or because God requires it; that is, whether we act from the greater or the lesser motive. It is the *motive* that gives tone and force to character. Conduct is secondary; motive is first. God is the only true motive for human conduct. The sublimest lines in English poetry perhaps are those translated by Dr. Johnson from Boëthius:—

From Thee, great God, we spring; to Thee we tend;
Path, *Motive*, Guide, Original, and End.

God the way, the motive, the guide, the beginning and end of all conduct—this is what is meant. Do you ask why it is necessary to take God into account, why it is not the same if we do right from any motive whatever? I answer it is all-important to get into the order and relation where we belong, the eternal and abiding order of God where right is right because it is God's nature and because it is the secret and method of the universe. Thus righteousness becomes supremely imperative; there is the whole universe behind it as motive; it lays hold of our inmost nature and binds us to duty by every law of our being. It is one thing to live in right relations to our neighbours because society and custom require it; it is another thing, not contrary but greater, to do right because we thus put ourselves in accord with God and His eternal laws. By acting from such a motive we rise into the heights of our being, and vindicate our nature as having its origin in God.

If the question were raised, What is the greatest achievement of man in his long development out of nature? or, What is the highest point he has reached? the answer would be *conscience*. No matter what it is, whether compound or simple, nor how evolved and produced, it stands as the high-water mark of human development. Beyond all the splendours of intellect or the achievements of will is this sense and play of *conscience*, this mysterious agreement of all the faculties which leads a man to say, "*I ought.*" Kant said that "the two most beautiful things in creation are the starry heavens and the moral nature of man." But the heavens are beautiful because they image forth the moral nature which rises above philosophy, reason, custom, and all else, with its inexorable, imperative *ought*—the greatest of words, because it stands for the highest action of our nature. If this most beautiful thing were to be seen in its highest form, I think it would be the heart of a young man when conscience speaks from its own dictate— before the years have furnished reasons and established habits. To see a young man settling a hard question simply because his conscience says "I ought" is the best sight this world has to offer; it is the order of the starry heavens fulfilled in the heart of a man.

I wish every young man could have inscribed upon his memory in unfading letters those lines of Emerson—

> So nigh is grandeur to our dust,
>   So near is God to man,
> When duty whispers low, *Thou must*,
>   The youth replies, *I can*.

But life must also be *godly*. Righteousness may seem to mean this, but the writer does not repeat himself. By *soberly* he meant an intelligent and earnest purpose; by *righteously* he meant fulfilling our duty to others; by *godly* he carries us a step farther. The first two terms refer to conduct; we are to act according to our real nature; but this tells us to act like God.

The thought is central to Christianity. Jesus had no other motive or purpose. What God was He would be. What the Father did He would do. As God felt so He would feel. To get at and into the mind of God, to be a true Son of the Father, repeating His life—that was the business He was about from first to last. He has no higher injunction than to be perfect as the Father in heaven is perfect. Tremendous truths which are hardly apprehended as yet, but how deep and true they are!

To get men into likeness to God, acting and feeling like God, thinking with God, like God in His love and patience, in the breadth of His wisdom, in the universality of His sympathy, in the steadiness of His movements, in His fidelity to His laws, in His loyalty to creation, in the peace with which He surveys His works, in His ineffable purity—if in these ways we become like God, we fit ourselves for sharing in His life, and we thus do share in it. For my part, I can see no other explanation of our blind world but this; if I can come into some sort of affinity with God I shall share in His destiny. Above and below all other laws we see this—that *like seeks like*. If I can become like God I shall go to Him; nay, I am already in Him, and I shall never perish.

There are many reasons for believing that God will keep all His creatures alive for ever, that He will never forsake any of the works of His hands; His whole nature seems pledged to this, but there is additional reason to expect it when in any of these creatures His own nature is reproduced. Then there comes into play the eternal law of like drawing like unto itself—God keeping His own because they have actually become partakers of His nature. To suffer them to perish would almost be like destroying a part of Himself.

Thus we see how thoroughly these three words cover the life that is set before us.

By *soberly*, we are required to cherish an intelligent and earnest spirit.

By *righteously*, we are taught to regulate our conduct aright in all our relations to our fellow-men.

By *godly*, we are directed to the world of the Spirit from which we came, and to which we may return with all the gains which a life so lived has wrought within us.

Character as Four-Fold.

> And every one had four faces; the first face was the face of the cherub, and the second face was the face of a man, and the third the face of a lion, and the fourth the face of an eagle.—
> EZEKIEL X. 14.

INSTEAD of trying to explain the nature of this vision, or trying to find out if it belongs to the supernatural or to the natural, let us first see if we cannot find some meaning in it. If we can find meaning, other searches are needless. So long as I find jewels in my path, I do not care how they came there.

The point most to be considered is not the nature of the vision, but of its symbolism. The way into the truth will be through that, and not through the action of the prophet's mind.

That which first strikes us is the

utter inconceivableness of the thing seen: whirling wheels under a cherub, hands filled with burning coals, fire taken from between the wheels and put into the hands of a man clothed in linen; cherubim with a man's hand under their wings; wheels and cherubim inextricably mingled; a wheel within a wheel, all forming living creatures, with backs and hands and wings and wheels full of eyes. There seem to be four combined into one, and each one had four faces—a cherub's, a man's, a lion's, and an eagle's. They mount up, cherubim and wheels moving together and standing together, "for the spirit of life was in them."

No sober mind can long consider this picture—hard as it is to bring under the eye—without coming to feel that real meanings are wrapped up in it. And one cannot long dwell upon it without beginning to see a certain coherence and logic in it that suggest a rational meaning.

It is well just here to speak of a peculiarity of Oriental symbolism as contrasted with Greek symbolism. The distinction is of value both in the study of art and of the Oriental religions. Religion runs naturally to symbols for expression; they are the language of the imagination; they express what we feel but cannot utter. The Greeks, in symbolising religion, conformed to art, preserving proportion and beauty, and using chiefly the human figure. They would not sacrifice art to religion, or rather they identified them. But the Hebrew, caring little for art and much for religion, piles up his symbolism without any regard to proportion or congruity or even possibility. The Greek symbol is made to be looked at; the Hebrew symbol cannot even be pictured; but, though not beautiful like the Greek's, it is more intellectual and far more religious; it tells more; its appeal is to thought. Take, for example, the symbolic vision of the Son of Man in the first chapter of the Apocalypse—hair like wool white as snow, eyes like flames of fire, a sword going out of the mouth, feet like molten brass—no beauty or congruity, but each feature standing for some moral reality or quality, and together forming a conception full of awful majesty. It is for the mind and not for the eye.

This is even truer of the vision in Ezekiel. I will not attempt to explain it further than to point out some of its correspondences about which there can be no doubt. If the source of the vision be asked for, we can only say that the mighty processes described in it are in themselves Divine and can have only a Divine origin. When we have the perfect we have the Divine. Let us not befool ourselves by insisting on definitions. Given a great religious nature like the prophet's, whose whole being was immersed in God; given his patriotism and the captivity of his nation amongst the heathen; given his faith in God as holy and just and the avenger of His people, and as a directing Providence holding in His hands the whole course of human events; given also those loftier glimpses and dreams of the exalted nature of man and of his relation to the lower creation, which strangely visited the minds of some great men of old as if born out of due time, anticipating what the later ages have come to know—given all this and we have the elements of the vision. The fundamental thought of the vision is that of *judgment*. The throne of God indicates that He is the source of all judgments, and that He directs their course. The throne is like a sapphire, its clearness imaging the Divine holiness. Next, there is a man clothed in linen, a human agent employed by God to execute

His judgments; next there are revolving wheels, the quick and sure movements of Providence, the revolutions of nations, the onset of armies. From the midst of them the man gathers coals of fire and scatters them upon the city. What is all this but the frequent page of history, told over and over again, and repeated even in our own day and generation? The vision is not an ancient dream, but a description of the French Revolution, of the war for the Union, and of wars and conflicts to come, growing up, as did these, out of cherished wrongs, and so incurring the burning wrath of the righteous God. It describes what is to-day imminent in the East, the judgment of God upon an inhuman nation. Here it might be expected the vision would end, but instead it spreads out into intricate forms, with close and subtle analogies and contrasts. The fire is not taken from the altars of mercy, but from the revolving wheels of God's judgments. The glory of God shines through a cloud of darkness; how true down even to our personal lives!

The introduction of the cherubim with their four-fold forms seems to widen the scope of the vision and to introduce new elements. They are incongruous in their make-up, and are associated with processes that seem intricate and complex to us, but they are simply the language of the age and nation, an alphabet of symbols, pictures of an idea. When great things or truths are to be told, the symbols necessarily are complex, as a profound topic requires a large vocabulary. But this vision is no harder to read, if one knows the symbolic alphabet, than is a printed page.

The cherubim stand for the people at large, for humanity as it is being purged and led onward through the judgments of God; for redeemed humanity; for the Church which God is leading through the ages; for the race in its ideal and perfected character, gathering up into itself the subordinate creation, working with the ever-moving Providence, moving when it moved, and standing when it stood. The truth here is—*God inseparable from the life and course of humanity.* The nation may be carried into Babylon, but God goes with it. He never rests in His on-moving; the wheels of His Divine purpose turn ceaselessly. The wings of the cherubim set forth the alacrity with which they obey His will; the hands under their wings denote efficiency and strength and action; the eyes that covered body and hands and wings and wheels indicate the wisdom that sees all things and suffers nothing to escape its use, all uniting to form a ready and strong and wise servant of God, by whom and for whom He is carrying on his judgments in the world.

Why and how the vision came to take so wide a range and to become so accurately prophetic of the course of the world, it is difficult to understand until we get some idea of the vast meaning that was involved in the symbolism of the cherubim. They stood for the mercy of God—winged, but human in countenance. If the question is asked, What is the meaning of this complex image taken as a whole? this seems to me to be the answer, It is the picture of a force, or a being, embracing all in nature below man, man himself, and God as the animating and directing spirit of the whole. This force or being executes the will of God. The wheels represent the forces of inanimate nature; the beasts represent the lower animal creation; man stands for the human force, the fourfoldness of faces and wings and wheels stands for universality and omniscience and instant action everywhere without turning.

Thus seen, it becomes a plain symbol that sets forth the eternal truth of God's sovereignty as it works out the great plan of creation. It is an early and mystically stated assertion that God directs the course of nations and of men, and that He uses the entire creation—the mechanical forces of matter, the brutes, man, and all that is in man—for working out His "bright design." It is a strange and mysterious bringing together of lower nature and of higher nature in man, who is thus made to comprise creation and is set to do the Divine will. Were the most recent conception of man put into symbolic form it would be like this. The newest truth is often the oldest.

The image suggests and resembles one more familiar in the

Apocalypse, the four-square city of God, the new Jerusalem, whose length and breadth and height are equal, alike incongruous and inconceivable image, but one that never fails to stir the imagination and to suggest the loftiest truths.

But that image is not fuller of suggestion than is this of the four-faced cherubim. They are, indeed, God's power descending from His throne; but it is vested in creational forms, and it is chiefly human; so that a sober Scotch commentator does not hesitate to suggest that it represents " redeemed humanity," though it would be better to say *ideal* humanity. As such, it stands for what is best and strongest and highest in humanity. It is humanity as God's perfected instrument for working His sovereign will in the earth.

Now, let us look a moment at these four faces, behind which lies the nature of man, or God's ideal servant. The face expresses the character. The true man will have, as it were, four faces, or four expressions merged into one—a lion face, an eagle face, a cherub face, a human face. What they express is plain—the lion face, courage; the eagle face, aspiration; the cherub face, contemplation; the human face, love.

There is hardly anything that one who has begun to take an earnest view of life more needs to keep in mind than that *true character is complex*. Just now the whole world is running to specialities. It is the vice of narrow thought, and the incident of complex civilisation. An ignorant man will think and live in the line of some one thing, and under some one trait, or impulse, or taste. It may not necessarily be bad: it may be good; it may even be religion, or what is thought to be religion, but none the less does it result in a narrow and ill-proportioned character. The complexity of civilisation seems to justify devotion to specialities as the only road to success or usefulness. The plea is strong—one object and total devotion to it; thus you get the strong and useful man. Yes, unless there is something better than the best in some special direction, unless full manhood is better than the best possible man in some one thing.

There is at present a serious danger in the sharp division of education into specialities, and one has not to look far before seeing its results. It has long been noticed that the study and pursuit of the three professions tends in each to produce a one-sided character—the crafty lawyer, the unbelieving physician, the over-pious minister; tendencies to be overcome only by broader studies. This influence is spreading through the whole range of education, with a seemingly growing readiness to suffer the special study or pursuit to shape the character into likeness to itself. The scientific men seem to care for little else but science; the economists care only for economics; the linguists only for grammar; or, turning to practical life, more and more are men losing themselves in their callings, which shape and colour them, give tone to their voices, expression to their features, poise to their body, until they become living embodiments of the thing they do. This, I say, is an increasing tendency. Men are far more intelligent than they were a generation ago, but it is a question if the "all-round" man is found so often as then, and if specialisation is not driving out symmetry and full manhood. This tendency is to be carefully watched in education; for man is not made for one thing, nor to be strong only in one way. He is the product of all previous creation; the primeval elements are at work in his blood and bones; the lion and the eagle are within him, and the living spirit of the eternal God has enfolded him and breathed itself into him. A man should recognise himself as such, and suffer his origin and his nature to direct his thought and studies, to prompt his reading and conversation, to lend dignity to his calling and to so subdue it unto himself that he can say, "I was not made for the calling, but the calling was made for me."

There is no more important truth awaiting recognition than that man is the summation of all previous creation. Hence, he is the expression of all that has gone before him. He is not only the outcome of creation, but the visible sign and word of it—a natural Logos. Carry the recognition into the moral world which lies open before men, and the true and perfect Logos will appear—One who is the very image of the invisible God, the first and last and full-born of creation, in whom the whole fulness of God dwells, because in Him creation, as it covers both the natural and the spiritual, finds absolute expression, and God returns to Himself in His perfect image.

This is the truth of truths. It will be the theme of theology for the next century. And it will be so confirmed by philosophy and science that it will be as unquestioned as gravitation.

It is true that we have our aptitudes, and that we should follow them; that society needs the trained specialist and the utmost he can give and do. Grant all this; back of it and above it lies the primal, fundamental and inexorable duty of developing our nature into its true proportions. The two things are not contradictory, nor difficult of realisation; or

CHARACTER AS FOUR-FOLD.   89

if so, then there lies the struggle appointed to us.

And what are these proportions that must be preserved at all cost? What are the things that a man must be and do in order to be a man? What must he have, whatever else it may be well for him to have? Certainly, these four qualities that form the faces of this symbol of the agent of Eternal Providence: courage, aspiration, thought, love. Let us look at them in their order.

1. By courage is not meant physical courage, nor yet moral courage. One should never be set over against the other. Courage is first lion-like, physical; and to it is added the courage of man, which is largely moral; the union yields true courage. It is made up of will supplemented by conscience and intelligence, one making the man feel that it is right to act or think in a certain way, the other to know it. It is expressed

in the upright form, the poised figure standing firm on the earth, the steady eye, the firmly-set features, the alert and commanding movement. Courage is a quality having no worth in itself, but only as a servant to other qualities. It underlies character, and without it there can be no character. It makes man a doer and achiever, and also, if need be, a sufferer; it enables him to live bravely and efficiently, or to die willingly for a cause. It is the quality that stands like a sentinel about personality, and keeps the man from lapsing into the herd about him. It is the quality that makes man the master of creation, and of himself; that leads him to undertake, and strive, and wait, and endure, and to conquer, if not in one realm, then in another.

2. The next quality is aspiration. One of the most important things for man to know is that he is the outcome of a creation which,

from the beginning, has groaned and travailed for his birth. If creation were conscious, it could be said to have aspired towards man; it has been at every step an aspiring creation. "The clod must think." The process must not stop with the creation of man. It must go on and become his prime function to aspire, to become more, to reach a higher life, to get into clearer light, to rise into something nobler and purer and better. It is the tragedy and the defeat of life when a man becomes contented, and has no ambitions, and is willing to live along on the same level of achievement or allotment. It is the tragedy and the defeat of society when it makes it necessary for men so to live—earning their bread only, and not taught or suffered to do more, or to think of more. There comes to every man at times—it is wrought into his nature—a sense of something above him, something great and beautiful and good, something that wins him and draws him to itself. He calls it God, he knows Him as the Creator, the source and end of all, the Father of his spirit; and in these better moments, he aspires to this God and longs to come into oneness with Him. When these moments come to a man, he is standing on the heights of his being, and is ready to fall into the Divine plans because he has risen to a comprehension of them. It is a sad thing to see a man without this aspiring quality, who sees nothing above him, who is content to live on the dead level of a finite world. Such a one has not awakened to his nature, or has smothered the sense of it. It is this quality of aspiration that keeps the nature fresh, that renews the faculties and makes them keen and strong for opening paths into the higher realms of life and truth. Without this quality, one plods along on the same dusty level, labour turns into drudgery; or, worse still, one becomes contented with things as they are, and takes on the colour and character of the finite world around him.

3. Take the next element, contemplation. Milton, who had studied well this great vision, thus refers to it in "Il Penseroso":—

> But first and chiefest with thee bring
> Him that soars on golden wing,
> Guiding the fiery-wheeled throne,
> The cherub Contemplation.

I mean more than thinking, more than any set use of the mind, more than intelligence. I mean thoughtfulness—the temper or disposition that lies back of thought—which is something higher than thought, and of more worth than knowledge—the brooding spirit by which one gets out of this world of sense into that inner or upper world of the spirit where truth has its abode. It is this that feeds and enriches and spiritualises character. Action, of course, is our first and chief duty, and the main lessons of life are learned through action; but as we need the night and its rest to give meaning to day and its labour, so do we need thought to interpret life. Run the Bible through, and you will find that the piety depicted on its pages has one constant feature—it is contemplative, thoughtful. There is no struggle after discoveries, no argumentation, no stress and hurry to get things done, but instead the contemplation of Divine things, dwelling on God, opening the mind to the Spirit. We do not think of Christ as striving to find the Father, but rather as resting in the thought of Him, and brooding on it; and the deeper look at St. Paul does not reveal him as a dialectician, but rather as one who meditated on the Gospel till it became a living force within him.

4. Look for a moment at the last quality—love, human sympathy. It needs no words to show that this is the crown of character. It is not merely a requirement of religion, but a requisite of character and selfhood. It is not a sentiment to be indulged; it is a law to be obeyed. It is not a soft and beautiful thing born in tender hearts, but is the rock that upholds character; it is the hooks of steel that bind it together. It is the common air of heaven and earth—the only breath that will sustain the human soul and keep it alive unto eternal life.

Now take a man, and lay on him these four things—courage, aspiration, thought, love: courage making him strong; aspiration making him earnest and keen and lofty and devout; thought making him wise and receptive of truth; and love the alchemy that turns life into

Divine power—and what sort of a being have you? Such an one as God can use in working out His eternal plans; one who will face all the four quarters of the universe and be ready for doing the Divine will in them all.

The only true conception of life is to do the will of God. Obedience is the secret of the universe. On no other plan can we live in this mysterious world, or find our way into the next. This is the meaning of the vision, and of all vision of God, and of all truth.

May God give us this four-fold energy, and so fit us to do His will, for through His will do we come into oneness with Him who is above all, and through all, and in us all.

Pity as Wisdom.

"And when He saw the multitudes, He was moved with compassion on them, because they fainted, and were scattered abroad, as sheep having no shepherd."—ST. MATT. ix. 36.

THERE are several ways in which we are prone to look at our fellow-men, especially when seen in the mass.

One way is that of indifference. They are going their own way on their own errands, and we are going our way on ours—what are they to us, and what have we to do with them? Another way is that of complacence. They are not harming us, and we have no desire to harm them; they have their rights; the world is wide; live and let live; let us be on good terms with one another. Still another way is that of contempt.

Taken as a whole men are so repulsive in their appearance and conduct, so abject and degraded in their ways and tastes, that it is difficult to keep the feeling down. Taken separately, we might find many to love and respect; and perhaps in any one of them we might, by searching, find enough to shut off any of these feelings. But looked at as a whole, seen as in the streets of a great city, or as massed on some holiday, they awaken in us a sense of separation that breeds indifference or contempt or easy complacence according to the bent of our nature.

It was not so with Christ. In Him we have an example of one who looked at men with a constant feeling of pity, never with indifference, never with contempt, never with simple complacence, but always with a deep, steadfast, abiding pity.

There was a great deal in the

age and in the condition of the people to call out this pity. The political condition was wretched. The people retained an intense patriotism, but they no longer had a national life of their own; the political order had been broken up and swept out by the Roman Conquest; they had become a tributary nation, were governed by foreigners, and oppressed by taxation which was administered by their own unworthy countrymen.

Their national constitution was such that foreign domination was peculiarly destructive of national life and feeling. Being theocratic, every feature and form of national life and procedure was religious, and now the whole was under the sway of a heathen government. Rome tolerated the national religion, but none the less did the foreign sway take the heart and soul out of the nation; it was no longer governed by its religion.

Thus it was thrown into confusion; it had lost its motive and regulator. The service of the Temple went on, but its essential functions as a governing force were destroyed. It was a legislature that sat but no longer governed. The effect on the people was to sink them in despondency. They had nothing to live for or to live by. The nation was hopelessly gone. The result was more than sadness. There is nothing that does more to weaken and break down character than the loss of national life, for the simple reason that fully one half of character grows out of and is fed by it. Take away this life, its constraints and inspirations, and personal character sinks and wastes away. Evil men come to the front. The great motives being gone, base and selfish motives take their place. The whole order being false and unnatural, the men who administer it become false and hypocritical and self-seeking. There being no general good to be gained, every man seeks his own good, and all the vices of selfishness have full and free course. Such are the evils when national life is interrupted, and such was the state of things upon which Christ opened His eyes. The nation was literally as sheep without a shepherd.

As Christ looked at this world so sunk in evil, so repulsive, so unlike Himself, He pitied it. Why did He not hate it? Why was He not filled with disgust by it? Why did He look on it with weeping compassion, almost condoning its sins, and breathing over it words of yearning tenderness and pity? Why, indeed?

I will try to indicate some of the reasons. There was one point on which Christ constantly insisted, one habit against which He steadily protested—namely, that of judging others. It was intimately connected with this feeling of pity. Christ was always logical; each feeling and thought grew out of another and supported it. The reason He pitied and the reason He would not judge were the same. In each case it was because He took the larger view. He would not judge because, looking on all sides, He saw that to judge and condemn was cruel and unjust; it was a verdict without a knowledge of the facts. In the same way He pitied the people about Him—unlovely as they were—because, taking a larger view of their circumstances, He saw that they were to be pitied rather than blamed. In other words, He looked at *causes*. This is always the mark of the thinker. Let the appearance wait; find out the cause, and then you may form an opinion and express a feeling. It was *because* the sheep had no shepherd that they were scattered abroad. It is easy and common enough to blame the sheep when they wander off into pastureless regions, where they faint for lack of care; but take the larger view—sheep were made to be shepherded, and if they are not there is nothing to prevent their wandering.

But Christ's view went beyond Jewish society. It is the wonder of Christ that in the little world where He found Himself He saw and marked the ways and laws of the great world beyond Him; that in the play of the human heart in the first century He disclosed its action in all centuries. He went deeper than external circumstances. There is more ground for pitying men who are entangled in evil than is to be found in the conditions about them. Christ went into the heart itself, into the whole being, and saw how it was made up; what defects and excesses, what bents had been given by heredity, what lack and weakness due to mistaken education; what deadening influences coming from poverty, what corrupting ones from luxury; how climate and sickness and accident have borne their part in perverting the man; and He saw also what a tremendous part is played in every life by what seems *chance*, whereby man is thrown off from the path of virtue—a chance word, a chance meeting, a chance temptation. There are fatal moments in life that fix its career. There are seeming conspiracies of Nature that thwart all good destiny. What goes on in that inner world where the fabric of human life is woven in darkness and mystery; what determining causes find their way in, what is left out or perverted or unduly increased, we know not. A misplaced atom in the brain makes all the difference between sanity and insanity; a slighter cause in antenatal days may give the lead and impress to character. Man is the final, the weakest and most plastic product of creation. He is a tablet on which Nature writes all her signs, he is wax which she moulds to any shape. He is the master of Nature, but before he comes into the mastery he is subject to the powers which he is to subdue. They play tricks with him, make him passionate with their heats, sullen and dull with their frosts, tease him with their uncertainties, mock him by their famines and storms, dwarf him by shutting him within narrow valleys, and subdue him to the fibre of the foods they provide.

Such thoughts as these help us to understand to what an extent the element of desert is to be left out in the estimate of any life, whether good or evil. Cause? There is hardly such a thing; when you attempt to assign it, it recedes and divides itself up into myriads of other causes, which go on dividing until they are lost in infinity. What makes a man such as he is? You do not know. If a chemist cannot tell how many forces go to make a tree and give it shape, much less can we tell what makes a man what he is, good or bad. He is the product of all that has gone before him, of all that is around him; he is a part of a great whole, and is the subject of its forces. But he is not wholly so. Over and above all these shaping influences is the great fact of personality—the will that says *I can*, the conscience that says *I ought*, the heart that says *I love*. They constitute a person; they make a character, and they are subject to judgment according as they act right or wrong. Grant all this; but it must be granted under the qualifications named. Personality is a real thing, but how hindered, how restricted, how overborne, how helpless even it often seems—a reed striving to hold itself erect while all the forces of the world beat against it.

Christ never overlooked or lowered the fact of accountability. He planted Himself upon the moral nature of man; but while He stood there and summoned men to repentance and duty, repeating His great commandment and pronouncing the doom of sinners, He saw the other side so clearly, and felt it so deeply, that His predominant mood was not one of moral measurement and critical award, but rather of excusing pity; the larger and deeper view prevailed over the immediate and superficial view. He did not part with His moral estimates; He took them up into a world of pity and love, where He bathed them in these gracious elements and then used them as saving powers. No! Christ did not overlook the fact that man is a moral being, that he sins and deserves condemnation; but He saw that this was not the whole of it. It is not the whole of a tree that it is perfectly adapted to bear fruit; it must have soil, light, moisture, and care. There has been far too much treatment of man as simply a moral agent, as a being whose whole action consists in doing right or wrong, and is to be registered accordingly. Theology has chiefly dealt with him as a sinner. A sinner he is, and the fact should not be minimised; but there is a great deal beside right and wrong that enters into his life. There is no gain in morality, nor in effectiveness of treatment, by regarding man *only* in the light of his main quality; nor is there any gain in dealing only with his nature and leaving out his circumstances. Theology is growing wiser in this respect. It is beginning to take a broad and an all-round view of man, and especially is it taking into account the world outside of him and the complexity of his nature as things to be considered. It is studying his condition as well as his nature, his history and antecedents as well as his moral make-up. Consequently, theology is now largely taken up with social questions and conditions; it is even becoming statistical, and is asking about wages and food and water, and houses and ventilation. It takes account of the debasing agencies around him, like the saloon and the haunts of vice, and in such ways it is making up its moral estimates. It is exchanging its doctrine of a fallen nature and inherited depravity for a doctrine of environment, and it finds the new doctrine much the more rational, and also more serviceable, because it tells one what to do. It is beginning to admit that men are not here in equipoise between good and evil, or with some inward, mysterious lurch toward evil, but that they are handicapped by external conditions, corrupted by their surroundings, pledged to evil by the very air they breathe. And thus there is coming into modern thought a pitiful quality from which good results may be expected. "The life of men unblest" is beginning to weigh upon the minds of their fellows. There are signs of a great humanitarian movement that will soon envelop us and draw us into its service. The Christian Church has always been humanitarian, but in blind and narrow ways, true enough or half true; but it has not yet clearly realised that it is called to undertake the redemption of society out of its *evil conditions*, and to create a world in which a human soul shall have a chance to live according to its nature. The movement has begun. It is the next step in that unfolding of the world which we call *progress*. Its origin and impulse have their

PITY AS WISDOM. 111

seat in Him who is over all and in all. The movement is God's, but men are its agents. It is largely helped and forwarded by science, and by the humanitarian instinct native to man; but what it specially needs is that quality of *pity* which filled Christ's heart.

This pity has in it elements of great power. It is wise; it takes the larger view, which holds us back from disgust and hasty condemnation and harsh criticism. It is not a weak nor a blind quality; it does not take the reins out of the hands of judgment; it does not ignore desert nor bar out punishment; but when all these things have had their due and done their work, it stays by—patient and yearning and hopeful. This pity is active and inexorable; it never gives over. It is love in its largest form—love lifted into wisdom and turned into energy. It is love changed into passion as it beholds misery. Christ lived and died in the full exercise of this pity. It was the sign and measure of His Divineness. It was the God in Him that made Him weep over Jerusalem. It was because His human heart beat as one with God's heart that He went about doing good. Hence his pity was powerful and redemptive.

It is very important to take this view of Christ, for the predominating quality presides over and determines the other qualities. However else Christ thought and felt, He pitied. It was this that made Him patient and forgiving and helpful, and especially it kept in place that tendency to judge which is strong in every moral nature. To condemn sin is high and great, but it is greater to pity it first and suspend judgment until it must be pronounced.

If this pity were to become a law and habit with us, it would work great changes in many of us.

First it would break up the critical and censorious spirit that is so common. What Christ calls *judging* is a wrong use of the moral sense—wrong because it lacks love, because it takes the smaller view, and because it overlooks the fact that we are all frail and erring beings in a world of temptation. What am I, what are you, that we should judge our brethren? The most critical are usually the most faulty; blind to their own sins in the degree in which they judge the sins of others. The opinion of a sound nature as to the bad conduct of another usually may be taken for granted. The loud and wordy denunciation of it, the expressed horror, the disdainful comment, the hard and cynical thrust—all in the name of virtue, and with something of truth, perhaps—do not reveal a high nor an intelligent nature; and they do not help to cure the evils they condemn. The reason why Christ so earnestly protested against the habit of judging and criticising was two-fold—first, that men might cure themselves, pluck the beams out of their own eyes; and then that they might rise to a higher grade of thought and feeling.

We cannot do much to help our fellow-men, nor to make them better, except through those higher forms of service which are urged by pity and sympathy. Love created the world, and only love can redeem it; and no true-seeing eye can look fairly at the world and see what a feeble thing is man as he struggles amidst its forces, swept hither and thither on its pitiless tides, safe only as chance or grace draws him within some peaceful eddy, but otherwise the victim of custom, passion, ignorance, poverty, and temptation in a thousand forms—one cannot take such a look at man without deepest compassion. His sin and lot might be mine;

perhaps *is* mine; nay, mine may be worse than his!

But pity means help. The need of the world is perhaps always at the highest point; still there are periods when the perplexities and suffering of the people seem to be unusually severe. All crises are times of trial. There is then the most disposition to criticise and condemn; the most need of sympathy and help.

Take the present industrial unrest—the symptom merely of a great social change that is going on under the development of society; one of its main features is the net of perplexity in which vast numbers are involved—forced to do what they do not approve, uncertain what it is right to do, pledged to principles which they know are only half true, and yet seeing no other way of gaining just ends; deceived, blinded, driven by necessity. No matter at which side of the industrial war we look, on either side there is the same perplexity of mind and almost equal weariness of heart. The condition is that described in the text: they are distressed and scattered, as sheep having no shepherd; they do not know what to do.

But the situation, for the most part, is calling out criticism and denunciation—labour denouncing capital and capital denouncing labour—one with a torch in hand and the other with a lash; neither side comprehending the helplessness or the exigencies of the other side; neither perceiving that both sides are involved in one of those great movements by which society is borne unto its destiny—a movement too great for the individual to contend against or to forward to any great extent. What it most calls for is patience and compassion, and the larger wisdom which they beget. In such movements neither side is wholly right nor wholly wrong. The truest view will be that drawn out of a consciousness that all men are brethren, children of one Father in heaven, over whom He bends in pity when they are in any way distressed or afflicted. It is then that Eternal Love girds itself for help and deliverance.

Reigning and Serving.

"And hath made us kings and priests unto God and His Father."—REVELATION i. 6.

THE Apocalypse has suffered more at the hands of commentators than any other parts of the Bible except Genesis and Daniel, books with which it has close affinity, Genesis because it furnishes so much of its imagery and thought, and Daniel because it is of somewhat the same character.

Indeed, the Revelation has been the occasion of so much that is wild, crude, and fantastic in the way of explanation that it came to be avoided, or was passed over as lightly as possibly, the least offensive theory of interpretation being adopted, but without much confidence in its truth. At no time, however, in later years has it been lightly esteemed; it may have been regarded as hopelessly difficult of explanation, but still as a treasure-house, barred but disclosing signs of unspeakable wealth. Or rather it has seemed like a sky filled with storm-driven clouds—dark, terrible, confused, but opening here and there in narrow rifts and letting in light of unutterable glory. The use and power of the book have consisted in phrases and detached portions which, by their beauty and pathos and by the spiritual truth and divine reasonableness lodged in them, have laid irresistible hold of men, and furnished them rallying cries in their conflicts, hope in their despair, comfort in their sorrow, and peace in death. Beyond this it had little use or value, and these parts were hindered in thoughtful minds by their close connection with what was so fantastic and wild; like lucid intervals in delirium, necessarily suspected.

But all this is passing away. A great change in Biblical interpretation has been going on in recent years; the difficult books have become easy and the simple books difficult. The most perplexing parts of the Bible to-day are the Epistles of St. Paul, because in them we have to deal with a great original mind, whose working we have not wholly fathomed, and whose relation to Judaism is not yet quite clear. But the Apocalypse is not theological nor speculative; it is imaginative and religious, and the parts that seem most difficult are historical and not prophetic. In order to understand the book one simply needs to get on the right track. The forest looks very dense, but there is a straight road running through it.

The reason for this change is the fact that within the past few years there has been a fresh and thorough study of the Apocalyptic literature that was produced in the century or two before Christ. It was a literature that followed the Prophetic writings, resembling them somewhat and bearing the same relation to the life of the nation. The Prophesies plead for a true national life, for righteousness as against the corruption that threatened to destroy the nation. The Apocalypses which began with Daniel and appeared under the titles of great names like Baruch and Ezra and Moses and Enoch—titles merely and not meant to indicate authorship—were always intended to revive the drooping spirit of the people by predictions of an overthrow of the forces of evil in one great conflict, after which the Messiah would appear and establish Israel as the head of the nations. They were political writings designed to hold the nation true to its conceived mission, and to lift it over its periods of depression and fill it with enthusiasm by picturing its future glory;

just as in all ages when nations pass through crises, the poets cheer and encourage the people by their glowing pictures of victory and glory. The poets of the Hebrew nation were the prophets and the authors of these Apocalyptic writings.

The nation was saturated with this literature when Christ came; and little in His career is more remarkable than that, while feeling the power of these great writings and in a certain way accepting them, He refused to think under the exclusive and material forms in which they were cast, declaring that the kingdom of God would indeed come, and come by conflict, but it would be universal and spiritual and within; not Jewish, not temporal, not external, not of this world.

This literature ran over into Christian times. Traces of it are seen in the Gospels and in the

Epistles; the writers could not escape its influence. As there had been Jewish Apocalyptic writings so there were Christian writings of the same general character. Nature and time and history were turned into symbols of the conflict which should usher in the reign of the Messiah and the glory of His kingdom.

There were many such writings, but the Church — not without reason—regarded them as dangerous, and ceased to preserve them. One—the Apocalypse of Peter—has recently been recovered.

Fortunately, the great writing before us has survived, and found its way into the sacred canon. It is as canonical as Isaiah, and for the same reason; it is full of inspiration.

I have said that this literature is no longer difficult of explanation; *we* now understand its nature and purpose. Its object was always to cheer and encourage the people in times of national distress, to keep alive the hope of a Messiah, and to impress upon them the fact that their hope could be fulfilled only through conflict. It was full of hatred of enemies, and was ecstatic in its forecast of the future. The key to one of these books is the key to all. The Revelation was intended to do for Christian believers what the Jewish Apocalypses had done for the Jews. It was intended to encourage them in their weakness while undergoing persecution, and to assure them of the final triumph of the Messiah's kingdom. Nowhere in the Bible, except in the words of Christ, does Revelation reach so high a point as in the first three and last two chapters, for nowhere else is there so clear a conception of the nature and course of the kingdom of God as in these chapters. They define, as no other writings of man do, the life of humanity, and they describe its destiny. By no other writers are we told so clearly what life is and what it will become. In no other writing is righteousness and its relation to the social life of man so clearly conceived and so sublimely expressed. There is no longer king or kingdom, priest or ritual: every man is his own king and priest. All things are new; former things have passed away. The smoke of appeasing sacrifice no longer ascends. A sacrifice that makes clean; robes made white in the blood of suffering love; life that flows like water out of the throne of God which is also a throne of suffering love—such are the prevailing conceptions of the book, and they are of the very substance of the Faith as we hold it to-day.

It also sets forth the hope which never forsakes the breast of man, that righteousness will finally triumph and the city of God be built on the earth, a hope which also includes our personal anticipations of a time when it can be said that "they shall hunger no more, neither thirst any more; neither shall the sun light on them, nor any heat. For the Lamb which is in the midst of the throne shall feed them, and shall lead them unto living fountains of waters; and God shall wipe away all tears from their eyes." Words like these have inexhaustible power and are eternally true, because they state an indestructible feeling and base its fulfilment on the triumph of Christian love. Men will hunger no more because the Lamb which is in the midst of the throne shall feed them. And they will weep no more, because God who made them will wipe away their tears—truths and hopes to be fulfilled in the perfect redemption of human society.

You have already perceived that this ancient phrase, "kings and priests unto God," puts us in the midst of the most modern thought. The phrase, of course, had its origin in the Jewish theocracy which combined government and religion. The king who ruled and the priest who ministered together constituted the administration which was neither political nor religious, but both. It was a governmental or national phrase, not an individual phrase. But this great Christian writer, retaining the idea of the phrase, discarded its general or political meaning, and applied it to Christian believers as individuals, calling them priests and kings; each one of you is a king and priest to God.

The transition from the old meaning to the new is tremendous in its significance. It assigns to man the place he is made to fill under the unfolding plan of God; it contains the secret of human personality. It shows what Christianity does with the individual, how it emancipates him from a system in which the government and the ritual take charge of his life, and makes him his own king and priest. The awful majesty and responsibility of the throne and the hierarchy are laid upon the man himself who is to reign and rule, serve and minister as though there were no nation and no priest. The phrase puts an end to all thought of a union of Church and State; to a Church clothed with political powers; to all notions of a Church as the vice-regent of heaven; to all intermediaries, saintly or priestly, between God and man. It says to the believer: think for yourself; be your own priest; let no one stand between you and God, nor between you and humanity. It exalts man to the pinnacle of his nature by making his highest duties matters of personal conscience.

The force of this conception

never had full power until the Reformation set it free. It became the soul of Puritanism, and is its soul to-day; and may God grant that it shall never die. Nor will it ever perish. It is impossible that man will ever permanently return to a lower conception of himself from which he has once emerged. Men may go on here and there as the willing subjects of a power that rules over them in ways unquestioned and undetermined by them, but it will not be for long. Men may still continue to kneel at altars where a hierarchy assumes special functions and special relations to God; this will linger long where it is traditionally and honestly held, for men are slow to learn and to change in religion; but where it a matter of imitation and sentimentality it cannot long last; it is like lighting lamps and pretending that it is night after the sun has risen. Man has begun to know himself, and he knows himself as a self-governing being, and he is also fast learning that he stands in direct relations to God, and that he is a full clothed and authorised minister and servant of humanity.

But the phrase is more than a definition of man's position; it is also a subtle definition of his duties; and here is where it becomes modern and practical.

I said that it puts us in the midst of the thought of to-day. This thought I conceive to be that *man is to govern himself and to serve his fellowmen;* two things he must do in order to fulfil his nature and destiny. They are the two poles of character between which the forces of his being play, and so produce the true man; he is to make the most and the best of himself; he is to do the most and the best for his fellow-men. Of what else is the world thinking to-day but this?

In order not to leave it as a vague generality let me try to indicate in what this reigning and serving consists.

It is, first of all, *self-conquest*.

It is a mystery of our creation that we are born in bondage and must achieve our freedom. The mark of childhood is subjection. We are subject to our emotions. Grief, anger, impatience, disappointment, fear—all have their unrestrained way with us. The passions announce themselves as tyrants; the mental faculties run wild. We begin life as slaves, not as sovereigns. Consequently, the first thing we have to do, the first thing a wise parent teaches a child, is to control himself, his emotions, fears, passions, desires, so that they shall not rule him, but that he shall rule and use them. The vagrancy of the thoughts must be corrected. The will must be subdued; the wild troop of animal instincts and desires must come under discipline and law; the passions must be curbed to their proper limit; the maturer forces—ambition, love of power and money and place; the lacks and perversions of qualities, such as indolence, timidity, indifference—all these must be brought under and so set in place that there shall be a proper balance among them, the man standing master over all.

> Man who man would be
> Must rule the empire of himself, in it
>   Must be supreme, establishing his throne
> Of vanquished will, quelling the anarchy
>   Of hopes and fears, being himself alone.

The highest mark of manhood is this condition of self-government, in which the man reigns over himself, holds himself steady, makes a phalanx of his powers, and so is ready for onset either by or against himself. Such an one is more than a true man; he is a symbol of a realisation of the world and of the whole order of God which stands fast and is fair and good because law holds it in subjection and compels its forces to work in harmony. Almost the highest term that can be applied to a man is that he is self-contained; he is his own world over which he rules in the name of God.

But along with this reigning is the other great quality—*the priestly element,* the ministering and serving quality. The training and culture of self; service for others in self-sacrifice—these are the two halves of the perfect character. They are not carelessly united in this great phrase —kings and priests unto God. They cannot be separated. The uniting bond is the words, "*unto God.*" One may be a king without being a priest, but not a king unto God. Human life is a divine thing. It has no coherence, no meaning, no use or end except as it is brought under the laws of God. A man does not *find* himself; he does not get upon the track of true living until along with self-culture he combines the rule and habit of service—making the most of others as well as the most of himself.

It is a very important matter, and one somewhat beclouded at present. There is an immense increase of self-culture. There are clubs innumerable in city and country for the purpose, and there cannot be too many of them, for knowledge and discipline lie close to the roots of character; but there is danger lest the other side be overlooked and neglected. Let us have all the self-culture we can get, but let it not be without the law of service. There is no form of selfishness so repulsive, so hard, so cold and desperate as that found along with self-culture when it does not open into and become one with benevolence. There is a good deal of it abroad, and its arctic chill is not infrequently encountered. Better ignorance, better untaught instinct than self-culture when it ends with self. It is self-defeating; for when one gets himself well in hand and begins to know himself, the question rises with imperative emphasis, *For what?* When one finds that he is a force the first question is, What shall I do with myself?

This was the question settled by Christ in the temptation. As the consciousness of the Messiahship unfolded within Him, He felt the kingly power and prerogative of it. Will He reign over and govern the people? Yes, but it will also be as a priest. In the spiritual clearness that came to Him He saw that one involves the other, that the ruling must be serving, *and that the serving itself becomes sway and power.*

It is fatal to keep them apart. Be yourself; become a king; rule over yourself; train yourself into a power that shall also govern others; bring out and make the most of all that is within you; make yourself strong and beautiful and masterful; but if you stop there, as there is much temptation to do, you will not have become what you were planned to become. Just as distinctly as one proposes to educate and cultivate one's self, should one also propose to train one's self in all those things that make one the servant of humanity.

These things will be chiefly moral and spiritual things; love, sympathy, devotion, self-denial, the humility that is one with service, an all-dominating spirit of helpfulness, faith in God, and that high sense of fellowship with Him in His eternal working, which is the joy and strength of all true-seeing children of God.

www.ingramcontent.com/pod-product-compliance
Lightning Source LLC
Chambersburg PA
CBHW030359170426
43202CB00010B/1430